Children's Bilingual A – Z Poems

儿童双语 A – Z 诗歌

By Mei Lan Wang

EduOrchids Inc

Children's Bilingual
A – Z Poems
For Grades K-6
English - Chinese

儿童中英双语
A – Z 诗歌
适合幼儿园至六年级学生

兰儿教育出版

EduOrchids Inc.

ISBN 978-1-9992858-5-2
Published by EduOrchids Inc., Toronto, Canada
First printed in May, 2021

Acknowledgement

A
Big Thank You
goes to the following photographers
for their amazing photographs:

Zhenqi Wang (China)
Zan Wang (Canada)
Xuebin Zhang (Canada)

衷心感谢
以下这三位摄影师
为本书提供精美的照片:

王臻祺（中国）
王赞（加拿大）
张学斌（加拿大）

Mei Lan Wang

EduOrchids Inc.

Letter Aa Poem

On a sunny autumn day,
ants go marching
under a big pile of hay.

Along the way,
they all say,
"Hooray! Hooray!"
"Finally, it is a good day!"

A
B C D E F G H I J K L M N O P Q R S T U V W X Y Z

字母诗歌 Aa

在一个阳光明媚的秋日，
一群蚂蚁列队前行，
钻入大草堆里。

它们一路走
一路喊，
"太棒了！太棒了！"
"终于有个好天气！"

A

B C D E F G H I J K L M N O P Q R S T U V W X Y Z

Letter Bb Poem

A B C D E F G H I J K L M N O P Q R S T U V W X Y Z

Buzz! Buzz!
I like the busy bees,
hovering above the baby tree.
They are making honey
to go with bread for my tummy.
Yummy! Yummy ! Super Yummy!

Zzzzz! Zzzzz!
I don't like the little brown bear
living in the big dark lair.
He just sleeps in his bear bed,
waiting for Brother Bear
to bring food to share.

字母诗歌 **Bb**

嗡嗡！嗡嗡！
我喜欢那些勤劳的蜜蜂，
盘旋在小小的树上。
它们在制作蜂蜜。
我可以拿来涂面包吃。
好吃！好吃！太好吃了！

呼呼呼！呼呼呼！
我不喜欢住在大黑洞里的
那只棕色小熊。
它总是睡在它的熊窝里，
等着分享
熊哥哥拿来的食物。

A
B
C
D
E
F
G
H
I
J
K
L
M
N
O
P
Q
R
S
T
U
V
W
X
Y
Z

Letter Cc Poem

A B **C** D E F G H I J K L M N O P Q R S T U V W X Y Z

When winter comes,
Captain Little Cat
likes to wear
a super cool hat.

When winter comes,
Captain Big Cow
likes to cover himself
with a magic cape and bow.

字母诗歌 Cc

冬天来时，
小猫警长
喜欢戴着
一顶很酷的帽子。

冬天来时，
牛警长
却喜欢披着
魔力披风作揖鞠躬。

Letter Dd Poem

A B C **D** E F G H I J K L M N O P Q R S T U V W X Y Z

Ducks play in the blue bay
in every bright sunny May.

Doves dance during the day
in every delightful way.

Dawn is closing in.
The sky is getting dark.
Dogs are barking in the park.

Dad is ready to spin
a game he really wants to win.

字母诗歌 Dd

五月，春光明媚，
鸭子群戏蓝色浅湾。

白天，鸽子翩翩起舞，
优雅舞姿人人喜欢。

夜幕降临，
天色渐黑。
狗儿还在公园里叫着。

爸爸准备就绪 要玩转盘游戏。
他很想赢下这一盘。

Letter Ee Poem

An enormous elephant
elegantly enters his room,
just to see an evil witch
on a magic broom
exiting the room
with a swift zoom!
"Zoom!"   "Zoom!"

字母诗歌 Ee

一只超级大象
优雅地走进他的房间，
正好看到一个坏女巫
驾着一把魔帚
一溜烟地
飞出去！
"呼--！" "呼--！"

A B C D E F G H I J K L M N O P Q R S T U V W X Y Z

Letter Ff Poem

A B C D E F G H I J K L M N O P Q R S T U V W X Y Z

In the fresh river,
a funny beaver
is swimming fast and freely.

In the fresh river,
a school of fish
are fervently finding their dish.

In the fresh river,
five little frogs
are sitting on five floating logs.

In the fresh river,
a big alligator
is busy splashing the water.

字母诗歌 Ff

在那清新的河里
一只可爱的河狸
轻快自由地游着

在那清新的河里
一群<u>鱼</u>
正忙碌地寻找它们的食物

在那清新的河里
五只小青蛙
坐在五根漂流的原木上

在那清新的河里
一只大鳄鱼
正在水中嬉戏。

A B C D E F G H I J K L M N O P Q R S T U V W X Y Z

Letter Gg Poem

A B C D E F

G

H I J K L M N O P Q R S T U V W X Y Z

Mr. Gordon
is playing his golden guitar
in his great garden bar.

Mrs. Gordon
is making a green toy
for her little boy.

Little Gordon
is playing gently
with his giant LEGO toy.

字母诗歌 Gg

高登先生
正在他的精品花园酒吧里
弹着他的金色吉它。

高登夫人
正在为她的小男孩
做一个绿色的玩具。

小高登
正小心翼翼地玩着
他的大乐高玩具。

A B C D E F G H I J K L M N O P Q R S T U V W X Y Z

Letter Hh Poem

A happy hare said hi
to a hummingbird passing by.
Then she hopped into a big lair.

In the dark lair,
the happy hare
saw a big heavy bear
sleeping in a high rocky chair.

She got so scared
and hastily hopped
out of the big dark lair.

A B C D E F G **H** I J K L M N O P Q R S T U V W X Y Z

字母诗歌 Hh

一只快乐的兔子
问候过往的蜂鸟，
蹦跳着进了一个大洞穴。

在漆黑的洞里，
那只快乐的兔子
看到一只笨重的大熊
睡在一只高高的石椅子上。

兔子吓了一跳
匆匆忙忙地
跳出那个又黑又大的洞穴。

A B C D E F G

H

I J K L M N O P Q R S T U V W X Y Z

Letter Ii Poem

A B C D E F G H I J K L M N O P Q R S T U V W X Y Z

I see an itsy bitsy insect
crawling with six little legs
on the top of an icy object
inside a box of pegs.

I see two interesting parents
with funny snow pants
carrying their lovely infants
dancing on the shiny ice.

What a happy family time! Quite nice!

字母诗歌 Ii

在装满挂钩的箱子里，
我看到一只六条腿的小虫
在一个冰冷的物体上
爬行着。

我看到两个有趣的父母
穿着滑稽可笑的雪裤，
背着他们可爱的婴儿
在闪亮的冰场上，翩翩起舞。

多么幸福的家庭时光！真好！

A B C D E F G H I J K L M N O P Q R S T U V W X Y Z

Letter Jj Poem

A B C D E F G H I **J** K L M N O P Q R S T U V W X Y Z

In January,
Jordan got a new toy
from his best friend, Roy.

It is a Jack-in-the-box
that looks like a jungle fox.

When Jordan talks to the box,
the fox pops out
with two jolly Santa socks.

Jordan likes to play this toy,
for it brings him a lot of joy.

字母诗歌 Jj

一月份，
乔丹的最好朋友罗伊
送给他一个新玩具。

这是一个盒子里的杰克
它的样子很像林中的狐狸。

乔丹一对着盒子说话，
穿着圣诞老人袜子的狐狸
就嘣地跳出来。

乔丹很喜欢玩这个玩具。
它给乔丹带来了无穷的乐趣。

A B C D E F G H I **J** K L M N O P Q R S T U V W X Y Z

Letter Kk Poem

In the Karate Dojo,
kids all know
how to do Karate kicks
with hands holding two sticks.

When they kick hard,
You can feel it in the yard.

When they strike up high,
they all say "KIAI (kee-ai)"

Kids keep doing the drills
until they master the skills.

A B C D E F G H I J **K** L M N O P Q R S T U V W X Y Z

字母诗歌 Kk

在空手道馆，
孩子们
都会手握木棍，
腾空踢脚。

当他们用力踢时，
在后院的人都会感受踢的威力。

当他们用力向上击拳时，
会齐声呐喊 "KIAI"！

孩子们不停地重复操练
直到技艺娴熟为止。

A B C D E F G H I J **K** L M N O P Q R S T U V W X Y Z

Letter Ll Poem

A B C D E F G H I J K L M N O P Q R S T U V W X Y Z

Little Lily
likes to watch lions dance.
Little Lily
likes to watch horses prance.

Little Lily
loves to leap like a frog.
Little Lily
loves to write letters on a log.

Little Lily
loves to play with ladybugs
Little Lily
Loves to give us lots of hugs

字母诗歌 Ll

小莉莉
喜欢看狮子跳舞。
小莉莉
喜欢看马儿腾跃。

小莉莉
爱学青蛙跳跃。
小莉莉
爱在木头上写字。

小莉莉
爱跟瓢虫戏耍。
小莉莉
喜欢给我们很多，很多的拥抱。

Letter Poem Mm

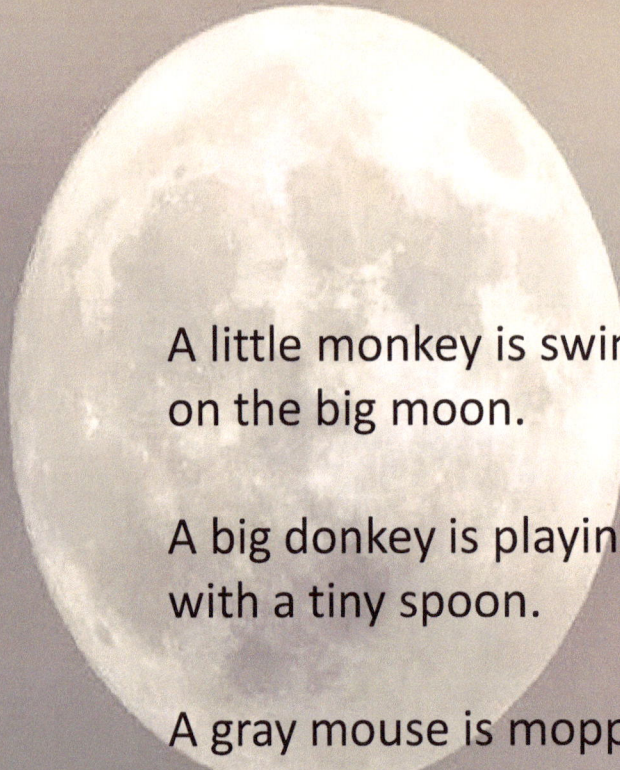

A B C D E F G H I J K L M N O P Q R S T U V W X Y Z

A little monkey is swinging
on the big moon.

A big donkey is playing
with a tiny spoon.

A gray mouse is mopping
in its green house.

An old man is cooking
with a big frying pan.

字母诗歌 Mm

一只小猴
在一轮大大的月亮上摇荡。

一只大毛驴
在戏耍着一把小汤勺。

一只灰老鼠
在它的绿色屋子里拖地板。

一个老人
正在用一口大煎锅烹调。

Letter Poem Nn

A B C D E F G H I J K L M **N** O P Q R S T U V W X Y Z

In the dark, dark night,
after Nature turns off its light,
in Room Ninety-nine,
a nice new nurse
is nurturing a newborn knight
who is chubby and bright.

What a quiet night!
Nobody is willing to say
 "Good night"!

字母诗歌 Nn

在一个很黑，很黑的夜晚，
大自然关了所有的光。
在99号育婴房里，
一个可爱的新护士
正在给刚出世的骑士喂奶
他圆圆胖胖，伶俐可爱。

多么安静的夜晚！
谁也舍不得道一声：
"晚安"！

Letter Oo Poem

A B C D E F G H I J K L M N **O** P Q R S T U V W X Y Z

There is one black owl
hooting on a green tree.

Under the tree,
there is a brown ox
mooing one, two, three.

In the river,
I see a swimming otter.

Near the river is my orange house
that has an orange couch.

In the house
is my mom wearing a blouse.

She is standing by the oven
cooking for a family of seven.

字母诗歌 Oo

一只黑色的猫头鹰
在绿油油的树上咕咕叫着。

树下
有一头棕色的牛，
哞哞叫着一，二，三。

我看见一只灰色的水獭
在河里遨游。

河边是我那橙色的家，
里面有一个橙色的沙发。

屋里穿着衬衫的那位
是我的妈妈。

她站在烤箱旁，
为七口之家准备饭菜。

Letter Pp Poem

A petit Princess Pig
is skating on the rink
with a pretty pink wig.

A Prince Parrot
is pecking on a big carrot
in a cage above the sink.

A priceless panda
is playing the viola
with her puppet Amanda.

A proud Mama
is baking a pizza
for the Party Cha Cha.

A B C D E F G H I J K L M N O **P** Q R S T U V W X Y Z

字母诗歌 Pp

小小猪公主
戴着漂亮的粉色假发
在冰场滑冰。

鹦鹉王子
在水槽上方的鸟笼里
啄着一个大萝卜。

珍贵的熊猫
跟阿曼达娃娃
在拉着中提琴。

自豪的妈妈
正在为恰恰舞会
烧烤比萨饼。

Letter Qq Poem

"Quack! Quack! Quack!"

A badling of ducks
are quarrelling around a rack.

"Hush! Hush! Hush!"

The Queen responds
in such a rush.

"Quiet please!"

"The princess
is taking a nap
under the quilt
on my Queen bed
that's newly built!"

A B C D E F G H I J K L M N O P Q R S T U V W X Y Z

字母诗歌 Qq

"嘎嘎！嘎嘎！嘎嘎！"

一群鸭子
围着架子争吵不休。

"嘘！嘘！嘘！"

皇后
急忙地示意着。

"请安静！"

"公主
刚钻到被窝里
在我那张新做的
皇后床铺上
午睡呢！"

A B C D E F G H I J K L M N O P Q R S T U V W X Y Z

Letter Rr Poem

A B C D E F G H I J K L M N O P Q R S T U V W X Y Z

At recess,
Rick was playing chess
with his best friend Kaine.

Then down came the rain.
Into the building, students all ran.

Right after recess,
the rain stopped.
And out came the Sun again.

Rick looked out the window.
There was a rainbow
above the willow.

字母诗歌 Rr

课间休息时间，
瑞克跟好朋友科恩
在下围棋。

雨来了。
学生们都跑进了楼里。

课间休息刚结束，
雨就停了。
太阳又出来了。

瑞克朝窗外一看，
柳树上方
横跨一道彩虹。

Letter Ss Poem

On Saturday,
I saw the smiling sun
spying me run.

In the run,
I saw a small duck wearing a silver sock,
sitting on a shining rock.

On Sunday,
I saw a sparkling star
smiling softly to a girl in the car.

I saw her sister
looking back at her son
in the mirror.

字母诗歌 Ss

星期六，
我看到脸带笑容的太阳
偷偷地看着我跑步。

路上，
我看到一只穿着银色袜子的小鸭
坐在在金光闪闪的石头上。

星期天，
我看到一颗闪闪发光的星星
温柔地朝着车里的女孩微笑。

我看到她的姐姐
在镜中
注视着她的儿子。

A B C D E F G H I J K L M N O P Q R S T U V W X Y Z

Letter Tt Poem

A B C D E F G H I J K L M N O P Q R S **T** U V W X Y Z

SEEKING WILD

Tiger, Tiger
One, two, three
Sitting quietly under a tree

Turtle, Turtle
Four, five, six
Freely floating near the sticks

Rabbit, Rabbit
Seven, eight, nine
Looking for a place to dine

Tina, Tina
Running with a hen
Then there are finally ten

字母诗歌 Tt

老虎，老虎
一，二，三
静静地坐在大树下

乌龟，乌龟
四，五，六
悠哉地围着树枝转

兔子，兔子
七，八，九
个个在寻找用餐的地儿

蒂娜，蒂娜
抱着母鸡跑
终于凑够了十个整

Letter Uu Poem

A B C D E F G H I J K L M N O P Q R S T U V W X Y Z

Uncle Unicorn
is wearing his unique uniform.

He is carrying an ugly umbrella
and a tiny cutie koala
on his upper back.

He is riding his unusual unicycle
up the hill
in a big storm.

He is going to a ukulele concert
performed by UFOs.

字母诗歌 Uu

独角兽叔叔
穿着独特的制服。

身上背着
一把丑陋的雨伞
和一只可爱的小考拉。

他骑着那辆罕见的独轮车，
顶着暴风雨，
沿着斜坡而上。

他要去听
外星人的小吉他音乐会。

42

Letter Vv Poem

A B C D E F G H I J K L M N O P Q R S T U **V** W X Y Z

A young violinist
lived in a violet van
with an old pianist.

The van always
parked nearby a big can
that belonged to a gentleman.

With a violet vest,
the violinist tried his best
to play some classical music
for visitors taking a rest.

字母诗歌 Vv

一个年轻的小提琴手
跟一位年老的钢琴家
住在一辆紫色的商务车里。

那辆车总是
停在
一位先生的大罐子旁。

穿着紫色马甲的小提琴手
绝尽所能
为休息的游客
演奏着古典音乐。

A B C D E F G H I J K L M N O P Q R S T U V W X Y Z

Letter Ww Poem

Looking out of the window,
we can see a beautiful world.
The cool April showers
always bring us bounties of flowers.

Looking out of the window,
we can see a musical paradise.
Chickadees, sparrows
wagtails, warblers
all singing us Edelweiss.

Looking out of the window,
when the rain stops
and the sun out pops,
we can see a beautiful rainbow
waving to us with his elbow.

A B C D E F G H I J K L M N O P Q R S T U V W X Y Z

字母诗歌 Ww

往窗外看，
我们可以看到一个美丽的世界。
四月凉凉的阵雨
总给我们带来鲜花簇簇。

往窗外看，
我们可以看到一个音乐的乐园
山雀，麻雀
白飞鸟，黄莺
都在为我们歌唱雪绒花。

往窗外看，
雨停了，
太阳出来了，
我们可以看到一道美丽的彩虹
用臂肘朝我们挥手。

A B C D E F G H I J K L M N O P Q R S T U V **W** X Y Z

Letter Xx Poem

A B C D E F G H I J K L M N O P Q R S T U V W X Y Z

My friend, Xavier
is a handsome captain
of an awesome airplane.

In his suitcase,
he always carries a blue iPhone
and a colourful xylophone.

At the security gate,
he never escapes the fate
of being detected by the super X-ray.

字母诗歌 Xx

我的朋友，尔克斯寨威亚
是一位英俊的机长。
他驾驶的飞机性能超棒。

在他的行李箱里，
他总放着一部蓝色苹果手机
和一个彩色的木琴。

每次过安检门道
他总逃不过
超级 X 光的扫描。

A B C D E F G H I J K L M N O P Q R S T U V W X Y Z

Letter Yy Poem

Yesterday,
in the yard,
Leo was playing a yellow yo-yo
with his friend Ray.

His younger sister Yohana
was working hard,
doing kids' yoga
with her mommy Tard.

In the kitchen,
his daddy was cooking chicken
and yummy, yummy bacon.

字母诗歌 Yy

昨天
在院子里
雷欧跟他的朋友若卫
在玩悠悠球。

他的小妹妹尤汉娜
努力地
跟妈妈塔尔德一起
做着小孩的瑜伽。

在厨房里
他的爸爸煮鸡肉
煎好吃，好吃的培根。

A B C D E F G H I J K L M N O P Q R S T U V W X Y Z

Letter Zz Poem

A B C D E F G H I J K L M N O P Q R S T U V W X Y Z

In the zoo,
I hear a pigeon saying "Coo! Coo!"
I hear a kangaroo saying "Peeka-boo!"

In the zoo,
I see zebras playing tag.
Zig-zag! zig-zag!

In the zoo,
I see monkeys chasing a broom.
Zoom! zoom!

In the zoo,
I see zookeepers zipping up zippers.
Zip-zip! zip-zip!

字母诗歌 Zz

在动物园里
我听到鸽子在叫"咕！咕！"
我听到袋鼠在说"躲猫猫！"

在动物园里，
我看到斑马在玩捕捉游戏
沿着之字形相互追赶着！

在动物园里，
我看到猴子在追赶一把扫帚。
呼呼！呼呼！

在动物园里，
我看到保育员们拉上拉链。
吱吱！吱吱！

My Personal Dictionary

Letter ___Aa___

ant _____

apple _____

_____

_____

_____

_____

_____

_____

_____

Letter ___Bb___

baby _____

bear _____

_____

_____

_____

_____

_____

_____

_____

My Personal Dictionary

Letter _____

_____

_____

_____

_____

_____

_____

_____

_____

_____

Letter _____

_____

_____

_____

_____

_____

_____

_____

_____

_____

Rhyming Words " <u>ay</u> "

Write each "ay" word in the blank.

day	
hay	
lay	
May	
play	
relay	
say	
spray	

Rhyming Words " <u>at</u> "

Write each "at" word in the blank.

bat	
cat	
fat	
hat	
mat	
pat	
rat	
sat	

Rhyming Words " at "

Write each "at" word in the blank.

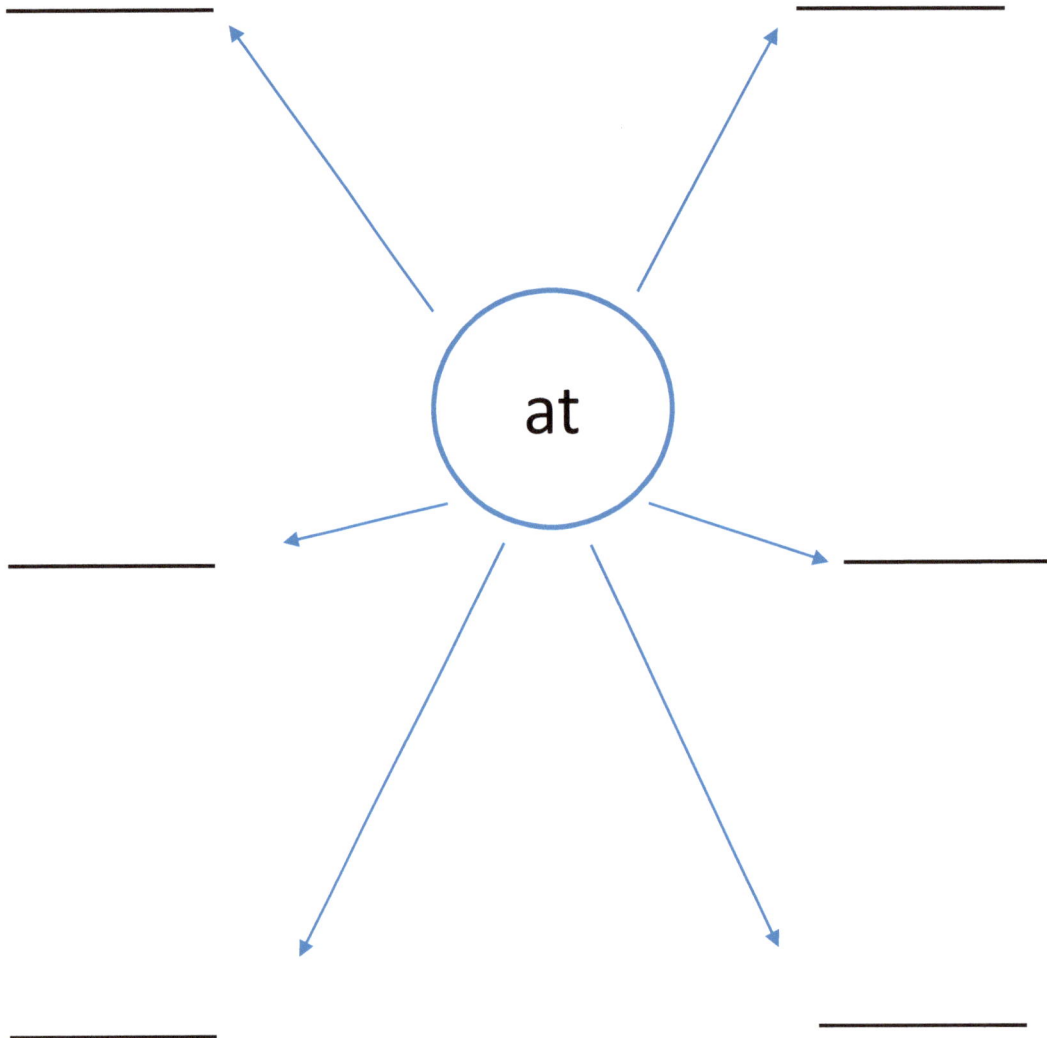

_____   _____

at

_____   _____

_____   _____

Rhyming Words " _____ "

Create your own rhyming words.

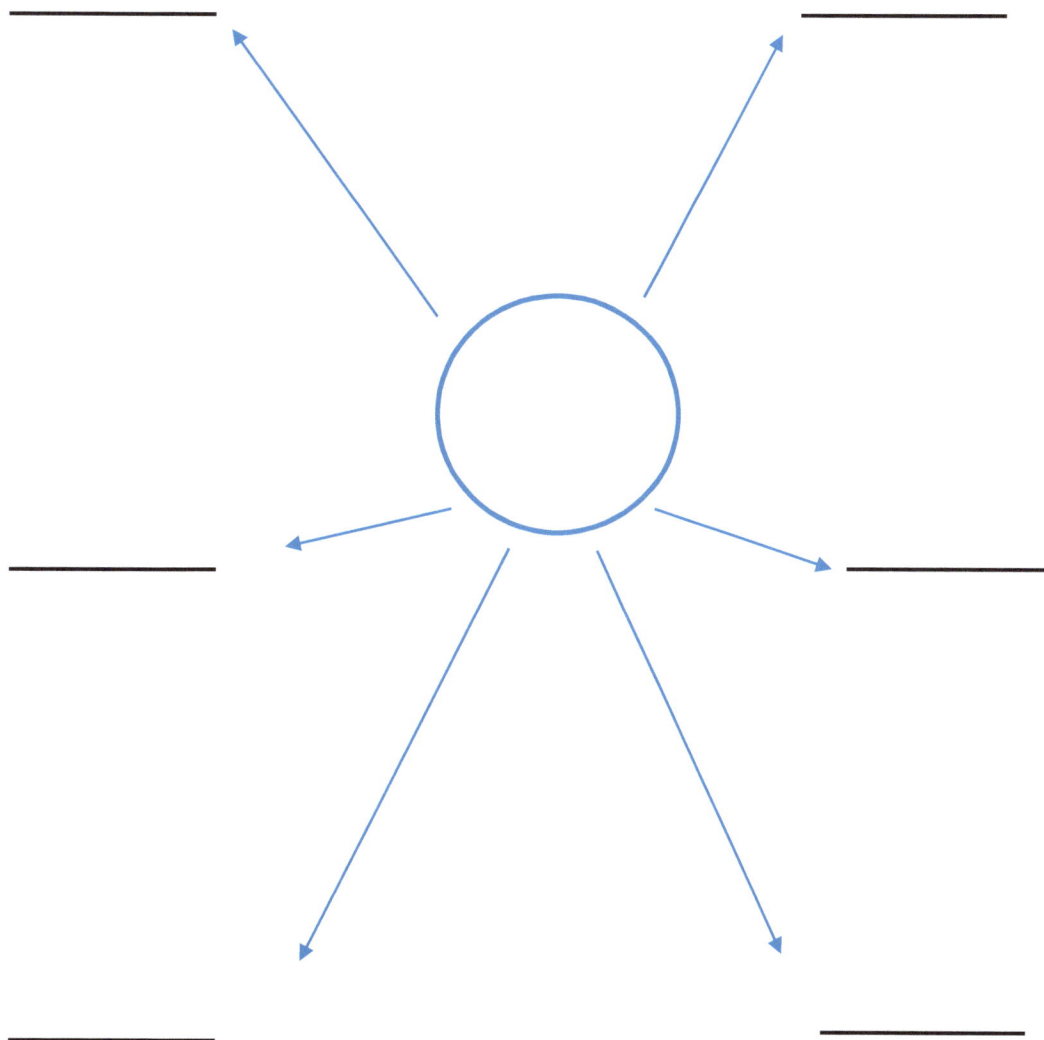

_____   _____

_____

_____   _____

_____   _____

Rhyming Words " _____ "

Create your own rhyming words.

Rhyming Words " _____ "

Create your own rhyming words.

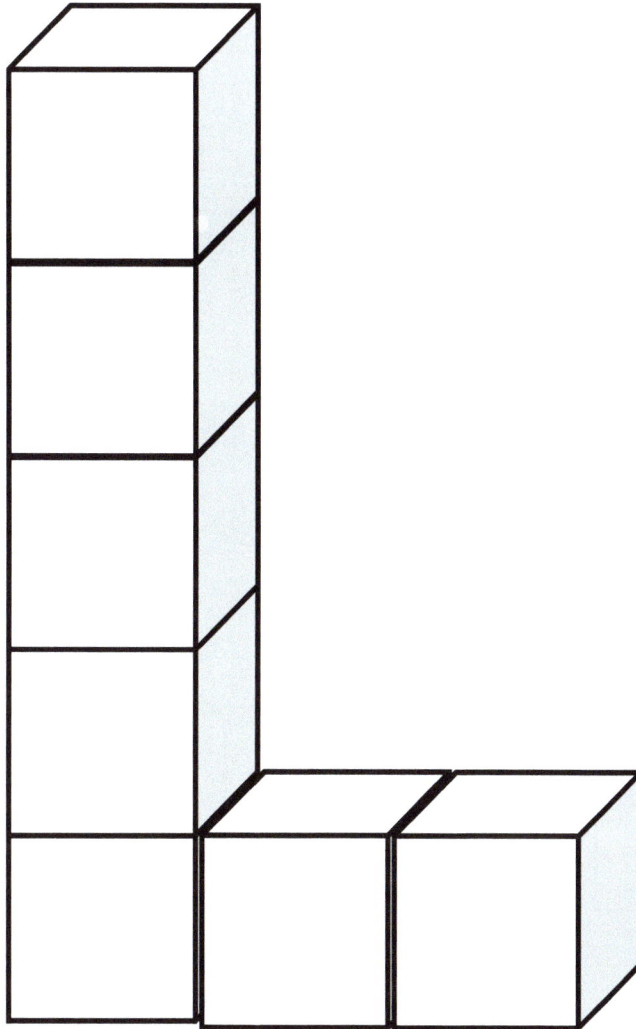

Rhyming Words " _____ "

Create your own rhyming words.

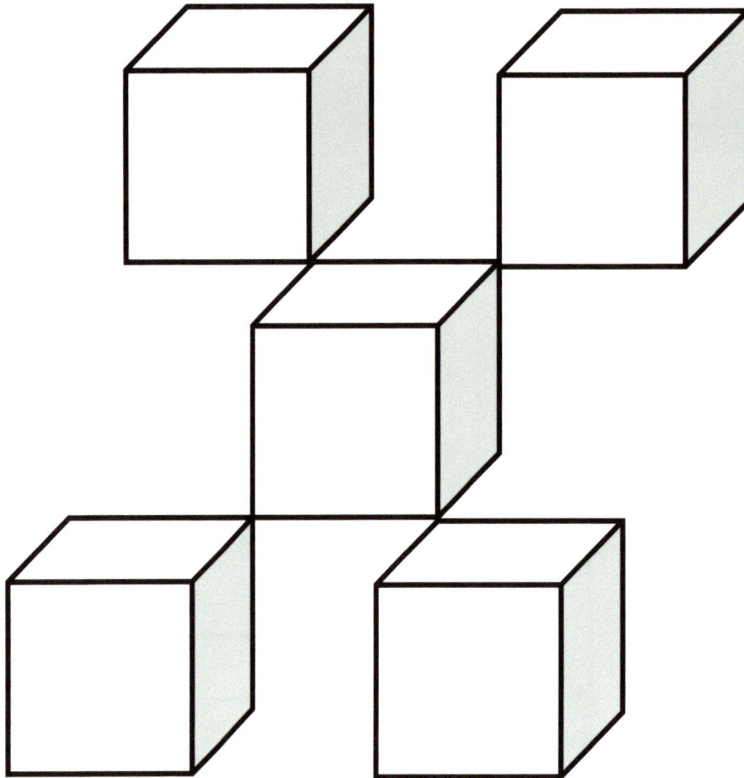

Rhyming Words " _____ "

Create your own rhyming words.

A B C D E
F G H I J
K L M N O
P Q R S T
U V W X Y
Z

Children's Bilingual A – Z Poems
is written for students
from **Grades K-6**,
who are learning both English and Chinese
languages.

Each letter poem includes
many rhyming words and animal names.

Rhyming words activities
are included in the book.

儿童中英双语
A – Z 诗歌
适合幼儿园至六年级
中英双语学习的学生。

每一首字母诗歌
包含很多英语押韵词汇和动物名词。

后面附有
个人词典和押韵词汇的练习样本

USD $ 18.99

www.ingramcontent.com/pod-product-compliance
Lightning Source LLC
Chambersburg PA
CBHW042016080426
42735CB00002B/76